SO YOU THI
7 PRACTICAL STEPS TO
E

Thanking with all my heart, Sunni and my Mum & Dad for their enduring support and faith in me.

I would also like to thank Joelouise, Ron, Dee, Sarah B. and Paul B. for helping to make this work's empathic gesture a reality.

All rights reserved. Except for the quotation of short passages for the purposes of criticism and review, no part of this publication may be reproduced or transmitted, in any form or by any means, without the prior permission of the publishers.

© 2001 Paul Hewitt

Published by Handsell Publishing

Cover design and illustrations by James Hewitt

Printed by Trio Graphics, Gloucester

SO YOU THINK YOU'RE MAD
7 PRACTICAL STEPS TO MENTAL HEALTH

CONTENTS *Page*

Biography	iv
Introduction	1
Roller Bi-Polar Ride	5
STEP ONE: Problem Recognition and Identification	9
STEP TWO: Acceptance and Resolution	31
STEP THREE: Tolerance and Problem Isolation	37
STEP FOUR: Physical Health Consequences	45
STEP FIVE: Stimulus Replacement, Encouraging Self-esteem and Motivation	55
STEP SIX: Overcoming Diagnosis, Institutionalisation, Medication and Social Stigma.	65
STEP SEVEN: Maintaining Health, Independence and Social Integration	79
One step at a time, the SEVEN STEPS reviewed	**89**
Glossary of Terms	103

BIOGRAPHY

Paul Hewitt was born in Australia to English parents who returned to the UK while Paul and his brother and sister were still young.

The family eventually settled in Gloucestershire where Paul attended the local Grammar school before leaving to take a degree course in Financial Services at Cheltenham and Gloucester College of Higher Education.

Paul left college after the first year, dissatisfied with his studies and wanting to seek direction and self-knowledge through travel. His sporadic journeying over the next few years took him to India, Egypt, Morocco, France and Wales where he worked, studied Yoga in the Himalayas, developed interest in healing arts and psycho-analysis - not all of which brought him the knowledge and enlightenment he had been seeking.

Paul returned to Gloucestershire after his roaming where not long after, he suffered a serious breakdown in his mental health. The account of his recovery became the rationale behind this requisite book of self-help.

Paul's interests remain concerned with the healing arts, the practice of Yoga, reading and the exploration of positive life-styles. He has self-published a small volume of inspirational poetry, continues to write creatively, enjoys walks in the countryside, attends to his allotment and likes tackling most home improvements.

INTRODUCTION

In a world of increasing social disorder and individual despondence it occurred to me that there is little practical advice offered in the area of attaining mental health, especially when suffering from the various psychological inflictions and diagnoses of today's social environment.

Having suffered some of these conditions myself I hope here to offer some practical guidance in the art of freeing the mind of self-inhibiting mental disorder. I have personally experienced mental states such as depression, suicidal tendency, mania, drug induced psychosis, delusions of grandeur, paranoia and other, socially unacceptable states that were none the less problematic.

There is so much we do not know about mental health conditions and I believe in part this is due to the degree of subjectivity involved in each individual case. Our problems are due so much to our individual experiences, environments, behaviour and upbringing that perhaps it seems there can be no help the individual can completely rely on.

In my exploration of mental health I have quite by accident stumbled upon insight and intuition regarding the acquisition of well-being. Many of these insights I have since had confirmed in my various studies in literature of the orient. I must admit though that some of this insight occurred to me under the duress of mania. I was fortunate not to forget this insight, losing it to the short-term memory loss that is sometimes a side effect of the medications used in mental health care.

I can only thank the long-term curiosity about the human condition since my teenage years for the current ability I have to communicate these matters. In spite of this comment about my current ability a lot of the realisations regarding my journey to mental health evolved out of common sense and compassionately applied logic. So it is out of this compassion that I discovered mental health and the subsequent physical, spiritual and environmental wellbeing. I also discovered that the methods by which I became well did not necessarily apply just to me but could be simply applied to any person suffering from any mental detriment. These conditions I discovered to be caused by erroneous thought forms and were the direct cause of my mental health problems. By erroneous thought forms it is meant, as is apparent in the coming chapters, those thoughts that are of a negative nature toward one's self or the kind of thoughts we automatically conform to, having actually originated in our upbringing, peer group or society and are not of our own independent making. These acquired, self-derogatory inferences act either repressively or oppressively upon our minds, resulting in the internal or external expression of disorder and psychosis.

There are different states or life spans of psychosis and so while one person may experience a one-off psychotic experience, another may have to endure a lifetime of affliction. Psychosis or disorder may also be caused by biologic deficiency in the brain, perhaps a condition inherited through one's genes. Other states of psychosis and disorder though are caused by circumstance, drug abuse and malnutrition or even through extreme submission or dominance in abusive relationships. These less clinical conditions for disorder tend to result in what is sometimes described as a 'blow out' case. This is where the psychosis is a temporary state caused by mental breakdown or acute confusion, resulting in a single experience of psychosis or episode of manic depression. These more short-term conditions may last up to two years or more and there is infrequently a return to disorder once relative health has been re-acquired.

The purpose of this book therefore with respect to the above statement is to act in those cases of 'blow out' disorders as a debriefing exercise, re-stabilising the mind and preparing the emergence of the fragile personality for it's tentative first steps back into community. For those sufferers of long-term clinical mental disorder my aim for this book is to provide a system for the management of disorder and hopefully therefore improved welfare.

It is my endeavour to keep this book from overly verbose description and rambling that may bore or lose the attention of those people I wish to aid. Keeping this matter as simple as possible is my ambition as it is simplicity itself that contributes mostly to my release from mental disorder.

ROLLER BI-POLAR RIDE

This chapter contains my personal description of the manic depressive experience I was ironically fortunate enough to acquire. At no point do I exaggerate any of the feelings and states of mind that were subjected upon me by this illness. In the following pages I aim to condense 18 months of continuous experience. Well, here goes nothing:

'All is quiet. I am standing in the toilet looking at the pattern on the curtains in front of me. Is that a face I see there? It looks that way, at me. What are these observations passing through my mind? Projections? I should not be thinking these things. Where are they coming from? A feeling of fear rushes through me. Where the hell's this stuff coming from? I'm not so quiet in my mind as I had witnessed, as I had thought.

'I could not have thought myself into peace; I did actually experience total stillness of mind, nirvana? I now notice myself describing once again. Descriptions, labels, projections, I've faked my peace of mind. They all think I've got somewhere spiritually enlightened. So up comes the mask I know to be false. You can't let on I tell myself. I stop talking to those I live with. I begin avoiding the others.

'Slowly I descend into a paranoid state, of course afraid to tell anyone about it. The feelings become possessive and I feel myself without a sense of knowing who I am. Am I a vent for the fear in humanity? Is it the unconscious fear within humanity or am I just afraid of what my humanity has become? Perhaps there is no difference. These intellectualisations do not distract me from my worry.

'Not eating became an attractive option. The mundane task of actually putting the food in my mouth seemed pointless as I was losing the will to live.

'Can't they see I am troubled, unable to speak past the choking sensations in my throat? I am sitting listening to someone honestly explain that he is somehow relieved that it is me suffering and not him. This seems honest and a little sadistic, but it doesn't help my dilemma. None here know how to help me and I do not appear to have a sane self that I know of to help me either. What I am going to do?

'I haven't slept for days with these insistent feelings churning throughout my head, heart and body. I can't tell the difference between them anymore.

'I am suddenly disturbed one night; shocked that something is pushing on my anus. Nothing is there, just the feeling of some force trying to violate (later I consider that this sensation might just have been cramp and I had at the time created a spontaneous and more dramatic conclusion).

'"Suicide. Got to be the only way out" I hear. "Suicide, suicide, suicide", can't stop that thought repeating on me. 'How long before I can't take any more? Actually do something stupid about it. It is dark here where I am rocking back and forth, trying to keep my body in that movement that I know is deeply my doing. I must not succumb to that impulse that wants to end me. I am worth more than that! SUICIDE! I tried twice to kill myself whilst the suicidal tendencies kept up their relentless imposition 24 hours a day for two months with no sleep.

'I had no choice but to eventually commit myself to the realisation that life wanted me alive for some purpose.

'I began to notice over the next couple of months a reduction in the amount of subjective fear I felt in relation to my environment and the people about me. This was a most welcome relief. In fact, so relieved was I that feelings of mild euphoria swept over me. It was as if the relative calm only felt so calm because of the hell I'd been traumatised with before.

'The moments of euphoric joy felt increasingly spiritual and almost in rebellion to my past silence I became invincibly verbal, unafraid to let my thoughts and feelings flow in endless adjectives, expecting to be heard.

'I felt strong, untouchable and free from worldly, mundane responsibility. Now the task of eating and drinking simply wasn't necessary, I am beyond all that! Little did I realise that my body had gone into a kind of automatic pilot and was feeding on my muscle tissues and waters. I carried out my thoughts in word and deed at an alarming rate, sometimes naked, sometimes dressed, whatever panoply tickled my fancy.

'My seemingly spiritual, free for all ended when I decided to find out which one of my fathers was actually in heaven. My birth father was at home and not in heaven. My Father's representative in one of the local churches I deemed to visit. He did not appear to be in heaven either, but giving the poor waif of a boy he found before him the freedom of his church for a few minutes gave me the boost my mania needed for the final push. Within an hour I was singing Kumbaya My Lord at the top of my voice in the local police station.

'My mania did not let me be shrunk by the shrinks when they finally arrived and by the time I was admitted at the nearest mental health facility I was no longer an anonymous individual claiming to be either Christ or his counterpart; to their credit and partly, I think due to a little synchronistic coincidence, they already knew my name and where I lived.

'Three weeks later after gaining nearly twenty kilos in weight and back up to my normal sixty-five, after sedatives, anti-side effect drugs, mood stabilising medications and consuming metals that make batteries last longer I began to wake to the reality that being under Section and held at Her Majesty's request was my current state of affairs.

'Three times in that year I was to find myself sectioned for various durations, finally resulting in the realisation that the system would only help me if I worked actively towards my own well-being. I had to find the motive for bettering myself in life and that turned out to be just that, bettering myself.'

Step One Problem recognition and identification. This chapter concerns itself solely with describing various mental disorders and their apparent sources making recognition of problems possible for the mental patient. Seeing afflictions in print can depersonalise a highly contentious issue for the sufferer, objectifying what is no doubt an excruciatingly painful condition.

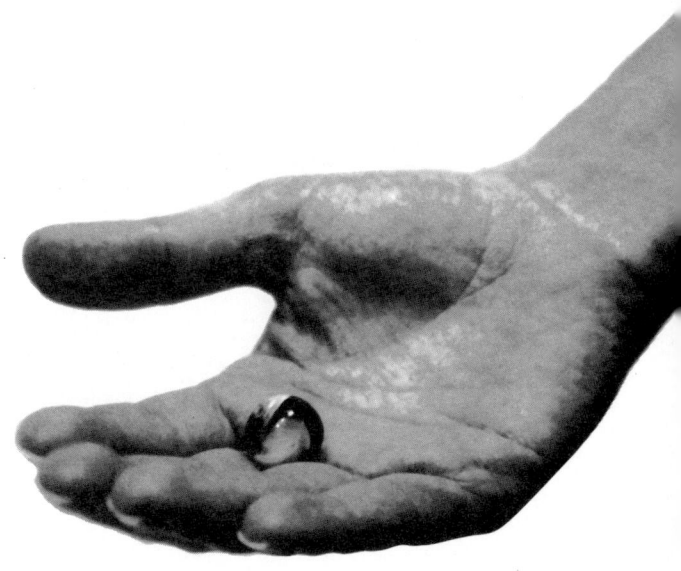

STEP ONE:
Problem Recognition and Identification

In the process of obtaining mental health it is absolutely necessary to identify and recognise that there is a problem. It is assumed that in receiving this literature you are wishing to increase your well-being. Therefore you have already turned the corner. Now it is up to you to complete this phase in life that requires of you to examine your own mental health, as follows:

If you do not have a carer you can deeply trust or a confidante you know to be true to you, best friend, lover or relative that you can share anything with, it will sometimes be helpful for you to make notes about the discoveries that relate personally to your life experiences of the past and present. For the future it is hoped that you currently desire peace of mind and a sane start in a new life. A life you can trust and have faith in.

Writing down our discoveries or communicating honestly to someone allows us to step aside from life when we feel it to be hurting us most. In stepping aside from our subjective life we can be objective about situations, mental states or any phenomena for that matter. We can then deal with these things through common sense (perhaps though it is not so common these days?). From this place of common sense or intuition we can rediscover our humanity, finding the compassion to increase our own or another's well-being.

Recognition

To recognise and identify our problem we must first be in a position to know that we indeed have a problem. Difficulties, no matter what they may be always let us know that there is a problem. Difficulties in communicating with others, traumatic situations where you are out of control, feelings of distress, fear, anxiety and paranoia or tendencies to self-harm are but some examples of the difficulties human beings may find themselves in.

Sometimes in your mind you may suddenly have an introspective moment where you realise or tell yourself that you have a problem or that something is just not quite right, that perhaps you need some help or that you would like to share something with someone but you just don't know how. Perhaps you feel that it would be distressing for others to hear about your problems and you use this justification not to tell someone or yourself that maybe you need a little help. This shows that you have compassion towards others and that you do not wish to hurt someone or trouble them with your problems. But please remember that you too are a person and this compassion is better served upon yourself, giving you the courage to tell others about your distress. Make that all too necessary first step in the right direction. It is important here that I stress the need for you to communicate with someone you absolutely trust will do the right thing by you. All too often people wish to help but can become a part of the problem and not a part of the solution.

Of course if there is no one you feel safer with than yourself then by all means do not fear to be alone in dealing with your problem. It is just that sometimes getting the words of our chests so to speak often lifts the load from our hearts, giving us the strength to make a new start.

If you are on your own and are trying to make sense of your troubles I have found having a pen and paper around helpful. You can talk to yourself without fear of getting lost in thoughts that can often run away with you. The kind of thoughts that often lead to those problematic feelings are all too much part of the problem. Keeping things in perspective on paper gives you a little breathing space. If though you are confident enough about keeping all these perspectives in perspective in your head and all at the same time then go for it. You'll be making up the rules for your own progress soon anyhow.

I am now going to expose some of the signs through which we can identify whether mental disorder *is* actually going on or not. I will try to identify signs of distress firstly in thought, then those signs that occur through speech and finally those that occur in physical action.

Exposition of signs in thought

This 'exposition of signs in thought' that expose detrimental health will be of little help to carers unless a patient is revealing to them the nature of their thought, otherwise this information is for those who are enquiring about their own mental health. Any thought has two creative potentials. One is where you find yourself thinking a description about your state of well-being such as " I am bad" or "I hate myself". These thoughts can potentially create the conditions of the thought itself. For example you might end up feeling bad, or feeling hatred. The other creative potential is that of when observing an emotional state that can then be consciously engaged, prolonged or dropped. This is where the first creative thought potential I spoke of comes in. You can affirm those states of thought or emotive mind that enhance well-being by repetitiously thinking the same thing. So, if you were to find yourself repeating the same thought you will tend to be prolonging that state which is being thought about. This may all sound a bit complicated, but it is quite simple, "you are what you think!"

Negative thoughts

Too many thoughts of a self-negating nature are inherently bad for you. They do not enhance well-being. They merely add to the sorry state of affairs that one is already in.

Fantastic thoughts

Thoughts of a fantastical nature are not necessarily dangerous, unless that is you believe the world and it's apparently solid nature can be manipulated to include your fantasies, incorporating and manifesting them at your will. This is potentially dangerous ground as you may be about to put your emotive thought processes into actions that are not currently physically possible in this world.

It is important that you can as an individual catch these thoughts in time to negate or do something positive about replacing them. Eventually any repetitious thought no matter how positive or negative it is will possess the mind to the degree that one will no longer be in humane control of one's mental faculties. The thought will find it's own way of continuing and you my friend will just be along for the ride. Once you start to think something often enough you may just get attached to the security of just knowing that you are thinking that thing. In this case you would be just creating for yourself the resultant effects, feelings and physical manifestations of that kind of thought. There is much you can do to end any chain of obsessive thought formation and this we shall make a start on in STEP TWO.

When we spend more time on and give more attention to thought than we do our other realms of experience, such as action and social communication, we can start to believe that these mental phenomena have more reality. When this happens our relationships with external phenomenon and social interaction suffer. This can lead to delusive and unrealistic perception of what you know to be reality, creating warped ideology and the resultant attempts at fulfilling impossible physical or psychic tasks. In fact we create individually how each of us relates to what is collectively known as reality. These apparently original or independent thought forms are often just inherited or conditionally acquired morality and value judgements fed to us through society, peers or family. It is through these thought forms that we relate to the world, define our relationships and accept our sense of identity.

Visions and voices
Other sources of thought-based mental illness may include surreal visions that suddenly impose themselves in the mind at unpredictable moments or perhaps voices that are heard internally as a sense of self but that seem to be not of that self, voices that tell you to do things or behave in particular ways. These voices and visions can be traced back to childhood trauma and coping mechanisms developed to overcome emotional shocks or emotional immaturity. The development of these seemingly

alien and strange voices is directly connected to lack of creative encouragement, trauma or abuse from our childhood; fantasy is then engaged and eventually the process of creating these strange voices becomes unconscious or second nature. The feelings that accompany these voices then become strange as the familiarity of their self-created origin is forgotten. The tracing of these mental incidences back to their origination can and often does relieve one of those experiences recurring. These realisations of the source of our mental illness spontaneously provide solace and healing when we are ready to choose a healthier mental attitude. With these realisations come the corresponding emotional outpourings that feel as though you had been holding onto them forever, things perhaps you could never have possibly shared with anyone. The kind of feelings that make you tired all the time. In fact, when you feel this recognition of emotional tiredness it is a good sign, a sign that you are approaching release and a time of good opportunity is arising.

Exposition of signs in speech
We come now to those signs of mental disturbance that can be identified through speech. Often we are prone to outbursts that require words for expression. Perhaps emotions that we have suppressed in the past are finding a vent in communication. These outbursts can take you by surprise as often they are out of their real-time causation. Sometimes we do not even know why we are feeling such a thing. The kind of emotional inhibition that leads to the necessity of these verbal outbursts is normally a result of unexpressed feelings. These feelings then turn in on the body and are internally expressed as increased emotive

and irrational thought forms, often resulting in physical tension, muteness, repressive behaviour and ultimately if not shared openly, to mental illness. One problem that I associate with verbal outbursts of this nature is that usually they require a listener and often there is just not someone around you can trust will emotionally contain you or who has the emotional wisdom necessary to hold you throughout. But if there is go for it! Speak your heart out. You will probably find your listener will have a growing respect for your honesty. If there is no one around for you write it down, just splurge it out on paper and read it over and over if necessary, get some self respect. It can be because of lack of self-respect regarding emotional honesty that we find ourselves mentally ill in the first place.

Nonsensical speech

The repeated occurrence of nonsensical speech is a dead give away for mental illness. Words dropped from or unrelated words dropped into coherent sentences perhaps suggest a cry for help. This happens where someone has been and still is disturbed but has not the emotional maturity or confidence in communication to express themselves adequately. These individuals just need a little support and trust to begin feeling assured enough to release their feelings. Another reason for word displacement can be that within the mind of the sufferer there is a priority, a mental thought chain currently in operation. Now, if simultaneously to this there is also some environmental need for communication imposing itself on the individual, like some authority asking a question the thought process interferes with this need, creating confusing feelings for the sufferer. This can lead to dropped words and incoherent, unrelated topic and speech manifestation. To the sufferer these displacements of speech may not be conscious or if they are noticed an uncomfortable wave of self-consciousness will ensue. This discomfort is due to the fact that the sufferer has unwittingly dropped their guard on themselves, revealing perhaps the obvious truth that they are suffering. This is not something they wished to show at all. I have watched this happen to me right in front of my nose and can empathise with those of you reading this that it is quite distasteful when you see yourself exhibit evidence of mental distress and incoherence.

Pressured speech

Another verbal dilemma for sufferers of mental illness is one that involves needing listeners to further delusive oration. A person exhibiting mania for instance often depends on others to retort regarding conversation. Replying to a "manic" often just "fuels the fire". Once the "manic" has tapped your ears he or she will continue for attention's sake, for the love to hear their own voice and the confirmation of the topics of conversation (usually topics inherently related to the delusive content of the "manic's" mind). This attention seeking is the "manic's" attempt to maintain and at best escalate their upward mood swing. A most desirable outcome but one that results in more so-called pressured speech and other typical manic behaviour. Pressured speech can feel dominating and disturbing to listeners. This is a little like the *"sympathy for the devil"* syndrome. Once the sufferer feels they are getting some kind of attention, even negative responses, there is a feeling of having conquered and behaviour is adapted in order to receive further attention. It can be the sufferer's inability to withhold contents of the mind that results in the free flow of verbal expression. Pressured speech has two sides. One is that it can be the escalation of mania. Secondly, the alleviation of suppressed emotion.

Exposition of signs in action and interaction
I will now endeavour to mention as many of the signs of mental illness that occur in action and interaction as I have either personally experienced or witnessed in others.

Insular behaviour where there is evident unwillingness to interact or communicate is a sign of someone trying to disappear in a self created world, safe and secure to the creator but is ultimately inhibiting and dominates that person's outward creative expression.

Fearful dumbness
Effort to speak is obvious, but tearful, panicked and desperate eyes give away the terrible emotional discomfort and constricting sensations of the throat.

Panic attacks are a sure sign of feeling psychologically unsound. They usually occur out of the blue when you think you should normally be feeling secure, safe and comfortable. Unless that is your anxiety is connected to some phobia or past trauma triggered by something from the immediate environment.

Rocking backwards and forwards in an attempt to remain in self-motivated physical activity rather than descend into a fearful lack of psycho-emotional control. Holding onto our bodies when afraid of losing ourselves is a coping mechanism. It is effective but enslaves one in repetitious movement. This coping mechanism also shows tendencies for fear of death (the wish to remain and hold onto body consciousness). This is a much unappreciated and little examined neurosis. Looking at the prospect of dying can be a beneficial tool for realising what we want out of the present and can help to gauge what we value. Of course I do not mean considering suicide as a way of escaping self- judgement.

Obsessive activity
Neurotic cleaning, eating or other obsessive, repetitious activity carried out numerously throughout a day is a sign of someone getting stuck in "safe" behaviour. This behaviour kills any and all spontaneous expression. Often this is another form of coping mechanism employed in an attempt to withstand a growing lack of emotional control. These and other repetitious behavioural syndromes are often the employment of a control mechanism, activated in order to not express a particular emotion. Confronting suppressed emotions and the remembering of the associated trauma can be very frightening for an emotionally inexperienced person.

Mania
Not stopping to calmly relax or sit down at any time is a sign of mania. Though manic action can switch to escalated thought processes that result in a relatively calm looking disposition, disguising escalating manic behaviour.

Fixation
Obsessive fixations upon various word types, allusion, sexual innuendo, numbers, nationalities or persistently

aping others are but examples of disordered behaviour and mental illness.

Dramatic body language regarding theatrical expositions of one's self-styled grandeur is a kind of performance that usually manifests when a willing or often unwilling audience is present. The willing and immature audience will usually encourage this kind of theatrical behaviour because it is entertaining, little realising that there is a person whose mania may be escalating to dangerous levels.

Grandeur
This is a sure sign of delusive thinking. Believing oneself to be a higher organism than other people can be a sign of suppressed pride. The release of egomania from its previously unconscious source feels irresistibly brilliant. This happens when in mania one's unconscious mental content spills out, uninhibited by the fetters of so called normal behaviour and conditioning. One is left in touch with enormous, uncharacteristically emotive potential or power. This deeply selfless, ego-less state of mind gets confused and mixed up with residual and previously unconscious personality traits creating a sense of comparative grandeur. Other people begin to appear mundane, afraid, inhibited and all that you are not. These other people and their sufferings tend to be forgotten as the best thing on earth is you, or so it is thought. In believing one's self to be higher there is always projection and the subtle judgemental sublimation of snobbery that puts others down.

Physical abhorrence
Shaking with fear when confronted with known associates or family members is evidence not only of mental disorder and delusive thought creation, but can otherwise be proof of abusive emotional familial practices.

Avoidance
Hiding under bedclothes for most of the day or believing that you alone cause the world's suffering are signs of depression or misappropriated guilt respectively. This can also be related to depression in regards to feeling safe and out of harms way in bed. This is a debilitating disorder that is sometimes caused by unconscious motives that inflict a torpor-like tantrum upon the sufferer. This is a very depressive state and is incredibly insular. Giving up on life and living as if dead is seen as a preferable state to be in. This is a sleepy malaise and with this and other dreamy maladies come ticklish, fuzzy sensations about the head, especially the ears, crown and nose.

Drug induced psychosis
Addictive use of illicit drugs to fulfil one's continuing psychosis is called drug-induced psychosis. This is a surprisingly common diagnosis. Psychosis is a state of self-induced fantastical derangement; disorders that are accompanied by hallucinations, delusions or mental confusions and loss of contact with external reality. This drug-induced psychosis tends to ensue out of fear of the mundane. As if a grounded and self-responsible life is boring and uncreative. Escaping the present in warped and unrealistic states of mind can leave one dangerously disconnected to one's healthy life rhythm, where beguiled by

an illusive pleasure we can induce psychosis, by far an undesired and unpleasant condition. Human beings have the tendency to use drugs in order to suppress their more primal drives as well as emotional trauma. As mentioned before, the persistent suppression of emotion can lead to escalated and delusive thought (implosive) or psychotic disorder (explosive).

Exhibiting animal behavioural patterns

This is a most uncomfortable state to fall into. Having limited or lost one's mental faculty for self-recognition it is easy to fall into and identify with mindsets that arise spontaneously from the environment. Doggish type depictions in deed are probably the most common form of animal aping. I believe there is a kind of psychic security involved in this kind of psychosis. It is safe to think and act like a dog, better than facing up to one's life traumas. These disturbing depictions in body language are an attempt to integrate the delusive content of the mind into outward behaviour and can be confused with demonic possession. It is also possible that some of these disturbing body languages are caused by spasms and convulsions induced through the prescription of anti-psychotic medications.

Self-harm

Self-harm is a little explored and inadequately researched form of mental illness or psychosis. Self-harm is a repetitive abuse inflicted upon the sufferer's body. It is commonly the cutting or burning of the body as a coping mechanism. Other self-abuses of this nature may be repetitious eating disorders, abusive relationships, drug abusing, overdoses or perhaps the creation of anti-social drama that cause the infliction of known punishment, ridicule or worse. The infliction upon the body of sudden intense sensation (which is all that severe pain becomes to the self harmer) is a method of coping that ensures the sufferer is returned to the body, or real time sensation. It is an escape from feelings and thought processes that are known to the sufferer to be the cause of their suffering. Hence we have with self-harm a "catch 22" scenario. To escape from the self-abusive thoughts and feelings that originated in the past one self-inflicts abuse upon the body or it's associated environment and interactions. This self-inflicted sensation becomes a pleasure for the sufferer as release and relief get associated with the action of self-harm. The pleasure experienced is the sudden release or in these cases diversion from the mental trauma. When any mental infliction is spontaneously eradicated what ensues is emptiness full of an illusory, peaceful assurance, comprehended and felt to be extreme relief. Another reason for self-harm can be that the sufferer feels so numb inside that they feel the need to inflict physical injury upon themselves in order to feel something, anything in fact. This emotional numbness is like depression and the sufferer feels inhuman and dead. Feeling alive in pain, remorse, guilt and sorrow is a better option than feeling dead, inhuman and a stranger to one's self, or so it is thought. Actually, to explore what we think and feel about death can be very revealing. No state can be inhuman, as one has to be human to experience it. And to estrange one's self from the superficial and expected behaviour of people and yourself can often be extremely liberating.

Suicidal tendencies

Suicidal tendencies and thoughts of a self-destructive nature are a sign of mental disarray. These dark and morbid, confusing states are the symptom of another state and are not necessarily the ultimate problem, though overcoming the tendency to kill oneself does often tend to be the priority. Addressing the motive and reasons behind these tendencies is the actual priority and is what can reduce the length of time one spends in "hell". It is possible to sit out the torment until, by the law that nothing ever stays the same and all things are subject to change, the states of destruction will pass away leaving one in relative peace, as I discovered. But this peace for me and I am sure for many others does not last so long. It all too often escalates into euphoria, hyper mania and finally into manic delusion. Often the underlying principle that causes suicidal tendency is aggression, a destructive influence. This can be turned inward or outward as violence. Self-destruction can express itself in submission to authority, degrading the self until it will have no choice but to fall into that emotional realm of suicide tendency.

Temporary psychosis

Psychosis can be caused by many temporary phenomena and so mental disorder can be temporary in nature. Shock, bereavement and drugs can induce temporary states of confusing psychosis. To be suddenly left in a state of mental disarray is a shock in itself, but psychosis or delusion can actually be an attempt at reclaiming some sense of mind. The process of creating delusional, perhaps fantastical psychosis can be the mind's attempt at formulating new structure, new identity. It can be the mind trying to reform, redefine character, constitution or mindset when it has been destroyed, disrupted or given cause to disorder. Most commonly it is a combination of the above and an unwillingness to incorporate new stimuli, accept a new situation or take responsibility for one's self. Mental illness can be a form of self-punishment or a vindictive decision on the sufferer's part to punish others. Descending into psychosis is often a subconscious choice, a way to escape something. The embracing of something new and healthy actually comes later when one falls out of love with mental chaos and it's resultant disorder.

Emotional naivety can also be a cause of mental illness. Being lead out of ignorance into situations that we are not emotionally equipped to deal with can provide the shock necessary to push one into psychosis. For so long there has been a lack of willingness to explore realms of emotional experience, as if feelings are not to be respected or trusted, that having emotion is weak. I guess I speak more for the male gender at this point. I call this malaise emotional degradation, an emotional torpor that restricts experience, paralysing joyful tears as well as compassionate ones. This all amounts to the lack of self-respect and emotional degradation that contribute to a growing sense of dispassionate dejection and hapless discontent, or in another word, depression. Looking up to others in lack of self-responsibility or selling out your own sense of empowerment or authority can also contribute to self-degradation, once again resulting in lack of self-respect.

Of course thought, speech and action are all interwoven and all contribute to a combined source of well-being, mental illness, psychosis or worse. We can treat ourselves and correct our mental behaviour in order to free ourselves of disorder. Ultimately it is you or I that must decide to make that first step, when it comes to choosing to be well. Whilst there remains an investment in the disordered behaviour or thought, whatever it may be, you will remain unwell. Whilst you find some security in the feeling that you create for yourself out of unhealthy mental or physical behaviour you will continue to feel and exhibit unhealthy tendencies.

There is a choice to be made on your behalf, by you and no one else but you. It is you who will be your saviour. There is help as and when you need it. There are places and people that offer aid, but it will only ever be help, it will never be done for you. You will have to do something for yourself. It may seem daring, perhaps confronting or maybe just pointless because you think you don't need any help, well if that is so, help yourself. Talk to yourself, observe yourself, get to know you a bit better, find out what makes you tick; what you are afraid of; what you want or need; who your friends are; take any action that is not out of those old patterns of confusion or distress. Take a calm breath, and change.

For those of you who are suffering and have identified this, it has not been my intention to condescend to know how you are feeling. But I have, I hope, given some solace with respect to at least having noticed and known of these terribly painful inflictions and faithfully shown that you are not alone in your heart. Many human beings have suffered what you are suffering and have either pulled their selves out of it or continue to manage their illness through healthy practices. I am sure there are many aspects and signs of disorder that I have omitted due to my lack of personal experience and observation. There are ways to help our selves that are universal and no matter how severe our inflictions are their effect can be minimised and in many cases eradicated completely. This is why I am here endeavouring to reveal some of those universal methods for self-help instead of harm. I helped my self so now know it to be true for me. If it can be true for me, it can be true for you. I will always refuse to believe that we as people are so different that we cannot agree in well-being.

In the coming chapters I am going to be dealing with practical ways of reclaiming mental health, a lighter approach than perhaps this first step but it is necessary to identify our illness if we are to free ourselves of it. You have to know what is ill before you can heal it. If you can find out how it is that you are not well, you will be left knowing how it is that you can be well. Once this knowledge sinks in you will wonder why or how you ever got sick in the first place. These wonderings continue to offer me well-being today as they constantly help me to align myself with what I know to be well. They also help me to avoid that which I have known in myself to be unwell. In fact once you become accustomed to affirming your well-being, which does not always take that long, your confidence will be such that in the future it only requires one or two positive thoughts to relinquish your mind of unwanted and unnecessary thought forms. This feels excellent as you start to recognise that one positive thought has more trust and less doubt involved in it than does the process of having to repetitiously plug something over and over in your mind. While there is felt to be self-doubt and a lack of faith in a better future then repetitious application of affirmation will be a compulsory factor in the early stages of self-bettering.

Step Two Acceptance and resolution. Accepting a problem relinquishes stubbornness and pride, those afflictions that often stop someone from ever getting the help they so desperately need. Once acceptance sets in there is the resulting resolution; the resolve to actually do something about one's mental problem.

STEP TWO:
Acceptance and Resolution

This step can take as short or as long a time as you wish. As simple as it may sound acceptance and resolution are crucial to the onset and achievement of the subsequent steps.

Acceptance
The resolution to achieve mental health will not come before you can find it in yourself to accept that *"OK, I am suffering"*. For me this realisation only took place when I had found myself for the third time held under *Section 3 of the Mental Health Act*. Seeing myself in hospital and needing to get out was the inspiration behind choosing well-being and not the mania that I had fallen in love with. Sanity to me meant neither depression nor euphoria, neither heaven nor hell, but somewhere in between.

I believe it is a kind of stubbornness or obstinacy that stops us from admitting to our selves even the slightest of shortcomings. Instead of humbly approaching change we decide we were always right, never wrong and surely not in need of changing our ways at all. This is pride. But out of this pride we can often do ourselves the greatest damage, refusing to admit to ourselves that we need help, even self-help. And of course out of pride we tend to be lacking in the compassion to even begin helping each other or ourselves.

So acceptance is crucial. How then do we go about it? Is it as easy as saying *"OK, I am definitely troubled. Friends and family are telling me. All the signs are telling me I have a problem. I keep getting into the same trouble. I keep thinking the same things"*. These are examples of what may be observed and thought when approaching acceptance. As soon as acceptance takes place there is immediate action regarding doing something about fixing the problem.

Admitting that you have a problem, even if it is only to yourself is enough to give the courage to start a process of change; to get up and out of your cloud of grey static that seems to float around when you are not feeling well, to make moves to clean it off and keep it off. This reminds me of something I used to do that started in hospital. When the common room would get sticky in the air with collective psychosis I would take my share and whatever or whoever else's had stuck to it to the shower and wash it off. It always worked, leaving me feeling fresher, better, and not just cleaner. Perhaps water is a good conductor for that kind of static energy that gets washed away down the sink; that bends running tap water when you put a statically charged plastic hair comb next to it. Aside from this it remains important to recognise that you are not the only person suffering. You are not alone in your pains. You may be physically alone but there is always the compassion in and around you for your journey to health.

We must not let those sometimes constant nagging questions like *"Why me?"* or *"What did I do to deserve this?"* or *"Why did this happen?"* get us down and stop us realising what we need in order to step further towards health.

These questions do have a place but not while they are part of the problem. They tend to cast the mind into reflections upon illness, never letting you be free of the pain. This is living in relativity to the past with a persistent question mark hanging overhead. When having got better you probably won't be like you were before you got sick. Getting better is not about getting well in comparison to how and who you were before you became ill. These comparisons only tend to confuse the process of attaining wellbeing and thinking like this will only lead to suffering and non-acceptance of the present situation. Besides, wellbeing I reckon is often just a fleeting state for most human beings. It is something I endeavour to maintain, experience and prolong by applying what I know to be true for me in terms of my health.

What tends to happen in the process of getting well is you do actually get the reasons why you became ill. When well enough to impersonally and objectively look upon your life reasons for one's sickness become clear through objective observation, not as answers to desperate questions. I'll share with you though one of the best explanations I have observed about my illness. It appeared to me that when some trauma or confusion leads to the breakdown or even complete halt to normal thought processes what can happen is any unconscious, stored up or unexpressed emotion, unresolved from the past suddenly becomes conscious. Now, this mixed up mental content, which is probably what makes dreams so surreal, suddenly imposing itself in the front of the mind and drowning out external reality makes living a very difficult task, especially relating to others in a coherent and rational manner.

Resolution

We come now to resolution. The word resolution to me suggests a solution happening again; to resolve; to solve again. It is as though we have been well before and know how to be well again. We just have to resolve to do it, making a clear resolution. And this is just as it sounds. It is crucial at some point to actually say to yourself in word or thought that you want to be well; that you want to better your self; that you are going to do something for yourself. Like get yourself out of this nightmare you've woke to find yourself in. These kinds of affirmation give courage in the times of deed that follow when it comes to reclaim your health. Even if you have always been sick, if you have never known a life of mental well-being, peace of mind is an option.

A firm resolution can become your constitution while it serves as a reminder for when you slip into those old patterns of behaviour. Resolution is the affirmation towards a better life, a life that nothing will stop you living, certainly no mental infliction that you can get yourself out of. The great *"I am"* affirmations are excellent for this. **"I am going to be well"** or **"I am going to better myself every day"**. An effective negation would be **"I don't want to be sick any more"**, taking empowerment away from mental disease. These empowering statements are fantastic for self-esteem. They give us hope for every day and for every tomorrow. They lead us into and through the process where we begin to replace those old sources of problematic behaviour.

Step Three Tolerance and problem isolation. Here one learns to tolerate the disorder causing lack of mental welfare without escaping from or denying it, culminating in the ability to isolate the problem, depersonalising it, objectifying and working with it in order to be free from it.

STEP THREE:
Tolerance and Problem Isolation

Having accepted that you have a problem that needs addressing you will now have to tolerate the initially constant recognitions of having this mental illness. By this I mean that you will feel a little plagued by your illness. For you will now recognise it's manifesting in your consciousness, in your mind and behaviour. This is a good thing. It shows that you have recognised your problem effectively. Sometimes you may only partially or incidentally recognise when you are manifesting illness, but any recognition is a start and is ultimately a step towards final mental well-being.

Tolerance
No doubt you will have had to tolerate your problem in the past, as a child perhaps, teenage adolescent, or adult, but what I am saying is this, you have probably had to suffer for a while at least with this distress. It is this tolerance that we are hoping to tap. Not in relation to ignoring or denying the problem, spending energy hiding and avoiding recognition, but in employing this tolerance in a positive way. This kind of tolerance will help you to enjoy healthier well-being whilst still exhibiting and attempting to control the particular problem that you have.

There is no failure with tolerance. Tolerance allows you to continue a relatively "normal" life while you are building the compassion to exercise steps towards mental well-being.

Thought flagging and labelling

When recognition is adequately acquired you can isolate exactly when and how your particular problem is manifesting. Then you can employ various methods to eradicate that problem, or at least to not behave or think in the way that you know causes you suffering. Once you are not thinking or behaving in those ways you will have eradicated your problem, at least in that moment. Though your infliction may manifest again and again you must not give up now. The added sense of failure or self-disappointment will aggravate your original illness. When you are successfully managing your illness you will begin to see brief periods where you are not expressing internally or externally traits of your problem. Basically this initial process amounts to recognising when you are thinking things that you know will lead to those feelings of despair, delusion or psychosis that you understand are unhealthy for your life enhancement. When these thoughts or feelings happen you will know that you must just watch and label them if necessary in your mind as the sources of your problem. This is the subtle recognition that you are not wishing to give these thoughts and feelings any more credibility and attention. Dwelling in these thoughts and feelings does not provide you with the security in sanity that you need to have if you are going to successfully lead a well life.

Practicing the above kind of mental thought tagging or labelling gives you growing confidence when recognising surprise manifestations of your illness. You can begin to live with your problem instead of your problem living and controlling you.

The flagging the appearance in your mind of thought trains accompanied by emotional recognition gives you emotional maturity and wisdom regarding your own mental processes. Ultimately this helps you to understand the thought process of the human vehicle. Something we all share. This all helps to build confidence in our selves and in the world about us, encouraging trust and enhancing faith.

This thought flagging has been a phase in my mental growth process that has helped me to recognise when I am going in circles in my head. It has allowed me to recognise earlier and earlier those thoughts that I know to be detrimental to my mental and emotional health. I guess it's about breaking habitual thought patterns. I have even applied this sanity to thought that does not interest me. Often I have found myself thinking things that do not really need to be thought but just carried out as an action. Or thinking things that I have thought already and am just going over again and again, blindly confirming original thinking and so on until I finally flag them, learning to recognise them earlier and earlier, until that thought doesn't happen anymore. This mental tool has freed my mind for activities that do interest me. Activities like exploring what love means to me, or actively seeking an assured sense of who I am regardless of extraneous forces.

Brain drain
To help confirm and isolate these mental incidences it can be helpful to write your actual thought processes down. This has been called *"brain drain"* and can be quite emotional when it is that you see your own mental content and the things that you actually spend your time and energy

thinking about. It can be very revealing. This writing exercise is another positive activity in your role as ambassador to your own health, another contribution to your growing self-confidence, attainment of sanity and emotional well-being.

These writing exercises, rather like writing your dreams down in the morning help to build up a more holistic, integrated picture of who you really are and perhaps who you really want to be. They reinforce your ability to recognise when you are investing your mind in activity you find unhealthy. If though you have a strong internal sense of who you are and what you want then these exercises are probably not for you and perhaps neither is this book.

Problem Isolation

In this isolation process the mental behaviour that we are holding out of our attention becomes starved of it's "life blood". This "life blood" is consciousness. What we give our consciousness to whether it is consciously, subconsciously or unconsciously is life, attention and the will for it to carry on, survive, adapt and remain. By reducing a part of your consciousness to ultimate insignificance you reduce it's power over your consciousness. This shifting of conscious attention and re-employment of conscious attention into other more healthy pursuits strengthens one's resolve and keeps whatever the chosen disorder is at bay. The effectiveness of this practice can only be fully employed when there has been absolute recognition and acceptance of the exact behaviour, mental or physical, that is to be denied power. This denial is not a burial of suppressed emotional experience hidden under inhibiting personality traits, causing repressive behaviour. It is the chance to live life with a steady and observable reduction in problematic mental content. This is a process undertaken in the fullness of conscious awareness; a conscious choice, not an unconscious removal of unwanted emotional responses initiated out of fear of those same emotions.

Step Four Physical health consequences. A person's physical health, body language and diet are addressed in this chapter. Vigilance in the watchfulness that is necessary for the sufferer's journey to health is a paramount factor in this step.

STEP FOUR:
Physical Health Consequences

Here I am going to try to convince you of the necessity of physical health and it's relativity to active mental welfare. For it is without this welfare you have found yourself in need of this book or know of someone for whom you are enquiring.

As you know the body does not last so long when it is neglected. When we spend more time and attention on the contents of our minds we correspondingly spend less time and attention on the upkeep, health and related necessities of the body.

There can be a balanced focus of attention or consciousness on all the aspects of one's life that are conventionally considered to be separate parts. If you were for instance to hold your body and mind, it's emotions and affections as all one thing you will soon notice that on no other part or relative separateness (i.e. Body, mind, soul, emotions, environment, inside, outside, etc) are you spending any more or less time, love, dislike or indifference. This is a peculiar phenomenon and it is those people dedicated enough to exploring mental health to ultimate fruition that will succeed in the realisation of this empirical statement.

But back to the task at hand, those physical health consequences. Our bodies and minds are more akin to movement than to static stillness and it is upon this movement that our ever adapting but sometimes repetitious mental illness and mental content depend. It is upon repetitious body language and posture that our mental formations are attached. I will be willing to bet that if you begin noting down not only what you are thinking but also how you are sitting or what you were doing when you had particular thoughts you will notice similarities, consistencies, consequences, order, perhaps even logic. At this point there often arises out of our memories the visions and cognitive origins of our sufferings. Far out eh?

Following on from the point of view of holding all things as the same you will find that through looking after the body the mind too is looked after. If you care for your mind you will find that the body too is cared for. If you take notice of your feelings and consider them you will begin to consider the health needs of not only your body, mind and heart, but so too the same of others. You will find compassion and self-confidence.

It is important that what you eat you find appealing to your taste and to the resultant sensations of you internal organs. For example, if your stomach aches after eating certain foods or you have painful, excessive wind or diarrhoea it is time to change your diet. Any excessive or obsessive eating disorder or habit will contribute to lack of mental well-being. Your body has feelings too you know, not just our hearts and egos. Our bodies know when we are abusing.

Sometimes we just get used to spending too much time in our heads, in a disconnected and unwholesome relative separateness. So much so that we lose touch with those other all-important aspects of human nature. We get used to denying our feelings, sensations, hungers and desires, preferring the cold world of rationalisation, constantly justifying our need to control.

All to often we adopt lack of consciousness about our bodies or our minds. It is easier to be ignorant. Who wants a hard life? Well I do, if it means being well, I'll take the hardest path. The irony is, the path that looks the hardest manifests the most pleasant or comfortably assured results, and conversely the path that seems the easiest manifests the most repugnant, ignorance inspired trials and tribulations. Apparent hardship usually just turns out to be rewarding challenge anyway. It is so easy to fall into a malaise of self-satisfied denial of welfare. This problem where appearances are deceptive is what often stops us making any changes in our life. We expect that this will happen or that will happen. We have so many assumptions about what we might have to do to get well or get conscious about things we've not bothered to enquire about before. It is our fear of change that stops us making any moves away from the security in pain that we have got used to.

The consistent postures that we embrace such as slouched or hunched sitting, hanging the head when walking, looking down at the gutter or any other body language that betrays self-dissatisfaction, depression, loss of self-respect or mania are simultaneously the foundation and result of defective mentality. By defective I mean that mentality which does not embrace calm assurance and enthusiasm for positive and spontaneous life expression.

Not only as in the previous chapter can you employ intervening thought measures (affirmation) to block defective thinking you can also employ different tasks, behaviour or body posture to eradicate mental illness. Once the habits are broken they are broken for good. Perhaps in the future you will be reminded of those pains you used to have by circumstantial stimuli, but this will only momentarily concern you as you know yourself to be free from your past, having employed your own methods to change your present and future health.

For those of us currently suffering from mental illness, who wish for some pointers regarding the halting of pain inflicting mental thought processes or imagery it is important that you make a physical movement, go somewhere new, do something new or different. Ask somebody to go with you if this is necessary or is a factor of your stay in mental health care facilities. If your mental pains follow you around focus your attention as purely as you can on the task in front of you. Make sure that this task is not related to your illness in any way other than as a distraction from your suffering. You may know this but soon you will not notice the application of distraction. Rather than purely distractive, the activities engaged in become positive, life-enhancing contributions to esteem. Your illness will be fading from consciousness as you give it less attention. The residual and subtle relativity to illness that is a hinder to the final stages of succeeding in leaving mental illness behind shall be dealt with in the successive step.

Perhaps getting some exercise if you know yourself to be sloth-like, constantly inactive and watching things on TV that do not stimulate or interest you would be good. Yoga, swimming, circuit training, drama workshops, try activities that channel all of your physical energy; that use all of your body and mind to focus and concentrate. These kinds of activities may tire your mind and body but this kind of tiredness is good as it encourages restfulness, sound sleep rhythms and calm composure.

What I am not implying here is that you become some kind of obsessed fitness freak or self-styled yogic guru in order to get well. Self discipline is OK as an aid to get rhythm back in your life if you lost it for a while, but if you give yourself a hard time for not achieving the goals you set because they are unrealistically demanding then you will again be just contributing to your distress, but in a different way. There is no point replacing one disorder for another.

Self-consciousness has constructive and destructive sides. Self-consciousness laced with fear, doubt or lack of faith will lead to paranoia, but self-consciousness enhanced with enthusiasm, esteem and motivation will lead to empirical wisdom and self-knowledge. So if you have the propensity for paranoia you now know that you have the same propensity for self-awareness, a great tool for considering yourself and others.

One tool for fostering introspection and the ability to step outside of my mental illness I discovered when I tried combining physical yoga with a kind of meditative practice. I tried holding my body still and straight when in bed. Whilst being comfortable but not too relaxed I attempted to remain absolutely still, except of course for the calm movement of my breath, deep and not fast, quiet and not laboured. What I found after a short period was that I became almost super conscious of my mental processes.

I was only distracted from mental observation when disturbed by heightened physical sensations. I found watching these processes but not getting involved in them a little disturbing sometimes but strangely this activity seemed to be releasing those thought patterns. Somehow in watching but not doing the thinking the thinking itself seemed to drain away leaving only thoughtless space. I found by not entertaining and having investment in defective thought routine I was increasing mental well-being and reducing my tendency to think unnecessarily.

The corporeal nature of the human condition loves order and structure that it can dedicate itself to. This does not mean repetitious behavioural patterns that breed discontent, lethargy, depression and "safe" behaviour. By structuring our day to include, as second nature things like regular meals and a pattern of rest or sleep that is equally regular we can enjoy the rest of our day as a journey of spontaneous creativity. These activities become our foundation for existence and create a balanced constitution. They provide the emotional neutrality that gives us the opportunity to feel the ups and necessary downs we need. We need these comparative, relative states of emotional transition to experience quality of life. This is the grounded "home base" that is our humanity. I guess it comes back to food and shelter at the end of the day. Take these away and mental disorder or confusion is never far away.

All I ask of you in this step is to have vigilance. The vigilance to watch out for yourself and what you know yourself to be capable of inflicting upon the your own mind. You can then do something positive about it. Being able to see what you are doing and retaining the ability to remain conscious in your daily affairs is what being aware is all about. If you can remain aware of yourself and your surroundings you can take control of your life instead of feeling that life is controlling you.

Step Five Replacing stimulus, encouraging esteem and motivation. Once behaviour has been adapted to cope with the removal of mental disorder with its own behavioural habits there is the necessity of replacing one's new but vacuous mind space with positive self image through affirmation.

STEP FIVE:
Replacing Stimulus, Encouraging Esteem and Motivation

Grieving lost behaviour
Because our minds have got used to the constant creation of our mental illness we get left with deep silences when we start to halt those unhealthy processes that perpetuate disorder. We can even end up grieving for the lost behaviour. There is nothing essentially wrong with this grieving for lost behaviour but inevitably this grief could leave you open to inviting that old detrimental pattern back into your life.

One other reason why you might grieve the loss of old behaviour is that it got you attention. When one is ill, loved ones and carers do a lot for us. They give us sympathy and compassionate service, but this is not for you to become solely dependent on. We can allow our behaviour to get out of control with respect to duration. Mental illness has a knack of living for itself, of finding ways to survive. Behaviour is a living presence after all, and who would deny a living thing existence? We tend to enjoy on some primitive level the receiving of this attention, but that is because being loved and receiving kindness is generally felt to be pleasant and enduring. Love *is* an enduring, even eternal life quality but do we possess it? Should we expect to get it whenever we want, especially if we're not giving a little too?

Emptiness

Empty mind space is a chasm for creativity. That space lives for to be consumed by thought, image, dream and many other attributes that constitute mental humanity. Mind space is the canvas upon which our imaginations perform. It is where we dream and where we often retreat to when feeling isolated, alone or abandoned. So rather like when one must get over the death of a loved one there is initially an adjusting to emptiness, a sense of lack, as if what you had lived for is gone. This is a problem with releasing mental illness, as it becomes a way of life after a relatively short time of entertainment. Once you are in that in between world of emptiness and lack it is easier to fall back into old patterns of familiarity, depression and behaviour. Easier that is than engaging one's innate creativity, starting something fresh in one's self. This freshness though is the only thing that will fully satisfy, giving fulfilment instead of lack. Lack will tend towards depression and loss of self worth, respect and esteem.

What we are concerned with here then is the replacing of this emptiness or lack with stuff that enhances well-being and gives you the reason to live again or to change old ways.

Self bettering

One great thing I discovered was the concept of self-bettering. During my mania I had become fond of martial arts and spinning things like sticks and staves. In my mania I believed I could tap the mind of any human being alive or dead and simultaneously exhibit their behaviour or expertise. I was often Bruce Lee, or so I thought. It was amazing though how this somewhat raw and unrefined belief gave me exactly the confidence I needed to be quite adept in a short space of time at difficult manoeuvres. One day whilst spinning a staff in the yard of the hospital I realised I was getting better at it. Of course practice does this, but I suddenly felt this could be my ticket out of here. If I better myself every day I'll soon be out of here. I will be better in myself. Better. Well in fact. I could be better and more well than ever before. Having tapped the confidence from the fact that I felt I could achieve anything I now saw all the obstacles in my way, anticipating the future and what difficulties I might have. I began to do my own social work; back dating social security payments no one thought I could. I was soon discharged from hospital and daringly; I felt, diminished my intake of medication. First went the anti-psychotics, then the mood stabilisers along with the anti-side effect pills, nothing happened. I didn't get spontaneously ill and end up back in hospital as others had fearfully predicted. From this time on I knew I was onto something. I felt myself to be miles away from other patients in terms of confidence, even perhaps better in myself than many people in society. Eighteen months, a book of poetry, a house and worthy employment later I find myself here at my computer finally writing down those things I knew I was onto back then when in trouble.

This book is my way of settling that troubled time of my past, finally releasing that phase of my life. I'll never forget but I know now that nothing in my present behaviour can ever be related to sickness and mental disease. I am now even able to see my previous disorder as having been a gift.

Again this step is similar to the last in respect to affirmation. It is about revealing to yourself that you are a confident, self-fulfilling person. Underneath superficial behavioural patterns you are positively engaged in life even if on the surface the entire world seems to be full of pain and suffering. Much of this though is your perception and not the reality of it. Our projections of what we believe the world to be are dependent on the content of our mind. If we want to change the way we see the world we have to change the content and therefore the motivation of our minds. Accepting the way the world is comes after you have learned to accept the way you are. Doing something about the way you are and so ultimately about the way the world is, is down to you. What would the world be like if we all tried to better our selves and therefore our environment too?

The moment you begin to replace self-derogative thought and the resulting behaviour you can, when sensitive enough, feel the difference, and if you can't you soon will, if you practice. You can feel the lightness coming in your body, in your chest, in your walk and in the way you hold your head. You'll find that you are less likely to take ignorance or no for an answer. You'll want to know why you are the way you are. This is when you suddenly get better and want to keep on getting better. Then there's confidence and the motivation to begin afresh. What an opportunity, a new beginning, a life without relativity to the pains of the past. Not many people have the benefit of knowing what that feels like. People who suffer mental breakdown and illness have this almost unique gift for new life, to being "born again" so to speak (no religious connotation intended).

I will add here though a little tip for those who suffer from mania and are at large in society. Channelling your mania into creative endeavour is excellent but it does not always free you from your mania, it just gives it a vent. Because you identify with say being an artist and it is your mania doing the identifying, it is easy in this artistic creativity to create symbolic reference to the ideology that supports your mania. It is useful to search out beneath those ideological reasons for loving your sickness what exactly is your motive for creativity. Creativity for creativity's sake may just be taking you for a ride and I would like to see you living for your own essential reasons and not pushed around by internal forces of self-deluding grandeur. I am not saying you should drop your modes of creative release but if you have not shaken that impulse to show off to yourself, internally dramatising your self-belief, then perhaps a little break from those illness supporting behavioural patterns would be beneficial. You can always come back to your passion later, refreshed, without craving or suffering lack of sleep from staying up to finish something you could not let slip encase you forgot by the morning. You could always make a note of it and get back to it after a calm rest.

Truth hurts
A reason why we sometimes resist taking a break from our psychosis is that we find it confronting. This confrontation point that we fear is that point when we realise something is wrong, afraid that we'll suddenly suss ourselves out; stepping out of ourselves in that moment to observe the truth of the situation. But as the saying goes "truth hurts". We avoid the truth because of the temporary pain it reveals. But it only reveals why we are in pain, it doesn't actually hurt, and that's the illusion. I would rather feel all

the pain of the world for a second than spend eternity inflicted by a fraction of that pain.

Self worth

Self worth is achieved when activity worthy of your love for it is actively engaged. What I mean here is stepping outside of your illness for long enough to discover activities that attract you, things you would like to do or achieve. These activities that you alone can conceive of and are attracted to are worthy of your love in the sense that you value them. The fact that you are attracted to other activities other than the disorder you have been suffering is a big signpost on the road to health. It is these activities that you must at all costs allow yourself to engage. Even if it requires a long term "game plan" you can give it your best shot, plan ahead. These goals will keep you grounded in days and weeks when you need a real landmark to steer by. Even when you get there or you find that perhaps you don't want that thing or that goal anymore it will have served you in the short term. It is still a positive achievement to realise that you don't want to do something. I often say that knowing who you are not is the same as knowing who you are. Knowing and guiding yourself through life by means of knowing and sensing what you don't want or need will keep you pointed in the right direction for what will ultimately fulfil you. The love to do what you want is important and we have here, I hope, been changing our attitudes of love to more daring originality and fearless expression, leading to independent enquiries into what we can achieve out of life.

Self respect

Esteem or self respect and dignity are achieved out of acts of sincere self love. You need love for yourself when you are in serious trouble. When you love yourself without reason you will find a growing egocentricity is your new mental illness. When sincerity becomes your reason for creating a you you can trust and believe in, you'll have found sincerity towards life and others, giving you value and a sense of self worth never before sensed. You are a valuable member of humanity, no less valuable than any other, no matter how self learned or ignorant you may be. Staying humble in this process of attaining self-confidence is paramount; we don't want dramas unfolding out of manic pride. Though I am expecting most of my readers have been humbled into humility by their oppressive illnesses and are unlikely to feel egotistically proud ever again.

Step Six Overcoming diagnosis, institutionalisation, medication and social stigma. In this chapter the forces extraneous to the individual that either help or hinder the journey to mental health are given an exposing evaluation.

STEP SIX:
Overcoming Diagnosis, Institutionalisation, Medication and Social Stigma

Identifying with diagnosis
For most sufferers of mental illness that have been diagnosed this very diagnosis can become a problem. Our diagnosis can become a source of identity. For example, *"Hello, my name is ..... and I'm a manic depressive"*. In the first step I explained how important it was that we accept our illness, but I do not imply that we accept our diagnosis. We must accept the characteristics of our individual problems, but the diagnosis can lead one to play straight into the hands of institutionalisation and all the fears that come along with that.

Institutionalisation
There are different kinds of institutionalisation and most of us identify this word with people who find themselves unable to live without being housed and cared for by the state; people who find it necessary to be cared for 24 hours a day. The problem with people who become institutionalised is that they *do* need help 24 hours a day. It is often a health trap caused and inflicted by the mind and it's tendency toward institutionalisation. But if we can help ourselves out of this mind trap, a security, which is often, ultimately unnecessary, we can free institutions of surplus patients. This will liberate funds to be spent on those constant additions to the mental health register. Discharging

ourselves from the mental health register and Sectional environment is a massive step and one that should be openly celebrated. It is of course an absolutely crucial step in being free of one's problem. As I said there are other kinds of institutionalisation; we can be institutionalised by medication, social services, social stigma and through self created security neurosis; and these too must be left behind or our illness adjusts, transforms and adapting to our consistent circumstances never leaves us alone.

Medicating Madness

When you enter into the acceptance of a diagnosis you will feel under immediate pressure to consume the various medications made available to you. I am not saying this is wrong but you always have the opportunity to consider carefully the consequences, unless of course being Sectioned requires of you that by law you must consume the said prescriptions.

Taking medication implies that you have assumed there is no other help available and that you trust the word of your GP when in vulnerable disposition. Now, when medication in the short term solves your mental crisis you become attached to the medication as the source of your well-being and lack of mental illness. When this has become well founded in your mind you will have become institutionalised through medication, in the sense that you will now associate well-being with medication and not with being inherently healthy within yourself. What ensues in the long term is fear for stopping the medication, another mental struggle comparable to giving up smoking cigarettes. Because your previous crisis is an unwanted result you continue to take the medication. Do you stop to consider that your well-being is psychosomatic, a result of no longer considering yourself to be unwell. This is an incredibly powerful affirmation, a frequently unconscious one at that. Not considering yourself to be sick directly contributes to well-being.

One thing I have omitted to talk about until now is the effect of medication upon the body and mind of the individual. If you have been hapless enough to discover the unsavoury side effects of medication then you will understand some of the things I am about to describe.

Here I have listed some of the common medications associated with the illnesses we are aiming to alleviate, obtaining my information from the *Good Housekeeping Family Guide to Prescription Medicines:*

Antidepressants such as Prozac, Seroxat or Cipramil are 'Selective Serotonin Re-Uptake Inhibitors' used to treat depression, anxiety, panic attacks and obsessive-compulsive disorders. Side effects associated with these drugs can be nausea, vomiting, diarrhoea, constipation, stomach cramps, anxiety, insomnia, nervousness, appetite and weight loss, reduced sex drive, dizziness, light-headedness or tiredness. Palpitations, shakiness, chills, fever, low blood sugar or fits are the more serious side effects that may occur.

Benzodiazepines such as Diazepam (Valium) or Temazepam are used to treat anxiety and insomnia, acting generally as muscle relaxants. Side effects can be drowsiness, light-headedness, confusion, forgetfulness, headaches, dizziness, blurred vision, rashes, low blood pressure, a dry mouth and urine retention.

Anti-psychotics such as Chlorpromazine (Largactil) and Haloperidol are commonly used in the fight against psychosis. They are used to alleviate conditions like schizophrenia, severe anxiety, and symptoms of mania such as euphoria or delusions of grandeur, agitation and other extreme behavioural disorders. Common side effects due to the consumption of these powerful drugs are drowsiness, dizziness or fainting, blurred vision, constipation, loss of balance, shuffling walk or stiff legs, spasms of the neck, face and back, trembling hands, trouble chewing, talking and swallowing, uncontrolled movements, weakness of arms and legs. These spasms, uncontrolled movements and stiffness are usually addressed by the additional prescription of a Benzhexol type drug such as Benztropine.

Benzhexol medications like Benztropine are used to relieve symptoms of Parkinson's disease and the side effects caused by anti-psychotic medication. The side effects though of this anti-side effect drug are: dry mouth, constipation, blurred vision, increased palpitations, dizziness, light-headedness, drowsiness, insomnia, nervousness and problems passing urine.

Mood stabilisers such as Lithium and Valproate are commonly used in the fight against mood swings in the manic depression illness bi-polar affective disorder. Lithium is also used in self-harming patients and Valproate (Epilim) is also used to treat epilepsy. The side effects of Lithium, a light metal also used in the manufacture of batteries are thirst, frequent urination, drowsiness, tremors, mild nausea, fluid retention and weight gain. Side effects of Valproate can be hair loss, over eating, nausea and indigestion. My experience of Valproate is one of extreme lack of emotional sensitivity; an emotional straight jacket.

Medication traps of consultant psychiatry

To show the difficulties involved in consultant psychiatry I will use myself as a case study and we shall see the kinds of medication traps we can get caught up in. I was admitted to hospital and quickly diagnosed as suffering from extreme but non-violent mania, euphoria and delusions of grandeur (though I did not consider it to be suffering at the time, not noticing my seven stone frame). I was immediately given Haloperidol and immediately went into spasms of the neck that within the hour it took the duty doctor to reach me had escalated, threatening suffocation. Then I was given Benztropine to combat the side effect. In terms of overall side effects I now have two counts of blurred vision, constipation and dizziness on my record and I am experiencing a shuffling walk (which doesn't sit well with mania) and loss of balance, bumping into the corridor walls. Some nervousness and light-headedness begins to set in over the next few weeks leading to a prescription of "sleepers" to help me sleep. The side effect stakes are now increasing and with the onset of another anti-psychotic drug, Chlorpromazine on top of every thing else I am now suffering from confusion, inability to read due to blurred vision, short term memory loss, migraine and a dry mouth. I turn to Benztropine as my saviour and spit the other "meds" whilst the nurses aren't looking. I become manic once again as the relaxing effects of the Benztropine enhance my euphoria. They try me on Lithium whilst maintaining the other drugs in slow reduction. Lithium makes me sick; to even get out of a chair made me throw up. I suffered this situation for over a week whilst being told that the effects would wear off. I didn't believe what I heard and showing my curiosity toward their *British National Formulary* I confidently requested an alternative. I was soon on Valproate, a drug for epilepsy that has the side effect of mood stabilisation. It worked, or rather it was whilst with Valproate in my system and passing green urine that I decided enough was enough and took the necessary psychological steps towards the confidence I needed to get myself well.

We can now see the dilemma facing psychiatrists in today's mental health care facilities. They can end up fighting side effects with medications designed for specific illnesses. The side effects become the illness or mental health disorder that is being fought. One drug to combat another whilst the patient begins to feel more and more isolated, without confidence in the system and experimented upon. Perhaps it is the medications that end up actually enhancing or disturbing mental behaviour, warping personalities or conditions into bigger problems?

Understanding, accepting and eliminating medication
Stopping your medication when you find no real reason in yourself to continue is an empowering reclamation of your independence, "independent of medication I am well". I do not at all suggest here that you just impetuously stop taking medication without considering the consequences. Look carefully at your own circumstances and apply some introspection. Enquire about how you became ill in the first place and then maybe you are in a psychologically strong enough position to attempt life without medication. You are

the source of your empowerment and never is something truly empowering outside of that. In association with the previous steps it is safe to cut down your medication as slowly or quickly as your confidence will permit. It is your confidence that should dictate your ability to control behaviour.

There is of course a place for medication and it is not my intention to advocate an anti-medication policy. Medications can give us the necessary opportunity of a chance to see life without illness, from where we can do something about our sickness. We can from a relatively healthy advantage point under the influence of medication choose the ultimate freedom, freedom from any institutionalised behaviour. We must as sufferers, patients or service users retain the consciousness that our GPs or consulting psychiatrists work through diagnostic frameworks that label and identify us through whatever information they can obtain about us. We must educate these people who hold large degrees of power over us, for our own benefit I must add, because it is our lives that they conduct and take responsibility for in our vulnerability. Be sure to tell your GPs and consulting psychiatrists everything you possibly can and make sure they are listening. Get yourselves educated about your illness or diagnosis. Look up your prescriptions in the *British National Formulary* (BNF) and find out the known side effects because you can have a choice when it comes to medication. The BNF can be found in local libraries or on the medications trolley of your hospital ward.

Social services
Your contact with social services can also be a source of institutionalised behaviour. Social services are an excel-

lent source of encouragement and therapy, often bridging the divide between insular behaviour and social interaction, but there must come a step beyond the security these services offer. Independence of these services is essential in your leaving mental illness behind. There are sources of life enhancing activity outside of social services and accessing them will be important in your future. Though financially I know there is an incentive to remain on the social services register, whereby you receive Benefits and free access to workshops, group therapies and other outpatient activities, it will become a necessary step for you to acquire the confidence to enter again the world of financial independence. If the necessity of making this step is overlooked you will feel a sense of unworthiness creeping into your heart as deep down you know there is a more independent life than social services dependence. Though if you are comfortable with these feelings and foster a love for them and an 'easy' but hapless life then you will be encouraging the much harder task of getting out of institutionalisation in the future. The longer you leave your independence in the hands of rules and regulations not of your own making the more your mind and body associates these conditions with normality, and so it gets harder to free yourself the more set in your ways you become.

Social stigma and labelling

Social stigma in the sense that I use it here is that kind of opinionated oppression that you may find yourself subject to, having been through psychological distress and the labelling process of the mental health system.

You will have at some time been diagnosed, treated accordingly and then pigeon holed by the health care system and in order to overcome these labels you must come to terms fully with your illness. All the steps in this book from 1-6 are about coming to terms with how you found yourself ill and how you plan to come out from around that bend, turn the corner and fulfil a more sane, healthy and wholesome human life. To see these labels in action on your life, used by social system in order to place you as a "this" or a "that", you must not be identifying yourself with the image. By this I mean some detachment is needed in order to be able to be objective about the stigma we are trying to eliminate. If you believe you are your diagnosis it will be harder to step aside from this identification for long enough to be able to be free to act independently of it. You must be independent yet understanding of the reason why those labels and descriptions are being used. It is not a great fight to free one's self of this stigma.

If you find yourself surrounded by people who will not accept you as having overcome your illness and got yourself well perhaps a little independence from those people is necessary. There is little knowledge at large in society about people who suffer from mental illness, so there is little need to be afraid of people's ignorance. Most people don't think too much about one another's welfare, being mostly too concerned about their own anyhow. You will find that once you start integrating with society in a well manner people will be surprised and astonished to hear that you were once mentally sick or Sectioned at all, saying *"I'd never have known it, you sound so sorted, so well"*. Now this is what I expect of your lives, those of you with the guts to make it, to take life by the horns, tame it and make it work with you. It is you who has mentally broken down that has the unique opportunity to start again, to be better than ever before, knowing yourself, having learned. You can feel young again from this learning experience instead of carrying that ageing tiredness that got you down and out in the first place.

It is your right to conceal your past as and whenever you wish. If you are trying to get on in life and there are obstacles such as moral honesty issues about whether you should reveal your past or not you must use your discretion. I would say that if your confidence is up and say, you're going for a job and you fear that there may be prejudicial consequences in being honest, I would not hesitate to conceal my past illness. Go for it! Get the job. No one need know. It is your confidence that gets you where you want to go. One little word of warning about concealing your past illness is if you still continue to take powerful medications that can affect your sight or coordination, you know the risks. If perhaps you need Housing Benefit and work is not coming easy then claim against the fact that you are entitled because of ill health. Make the system work for you until you are absolutely ready. Mental illness, as with other illnesses is held highly confidential by departments of health and social services.

Confident communication
You'll probably find that when you feel comfortable enough in conversation with someone and they ask a particular question and feeling it unavoidable that you say something of your past, be honest. Tell what you can. These moments of candid honesty help to clear your heart and mind of any residual, self conscious inhibitions regarding your past or your illness. People tend to have more respect for your

honesty when they see how easily you communicate about vulnerable subjects, talking at ease about personal matters more effectively perhaps than they do about their own.

Confidence can be found in many things the more aware you are prepared to be of yourself and the direction that you wish to take.

Step Seven Maintaining health, independence and social integration. This chapter asks of individuals concerned to maintain vigilance in the application of the previous steps in order to maintain well-being and to achieve a future where mental disorder is not an option.

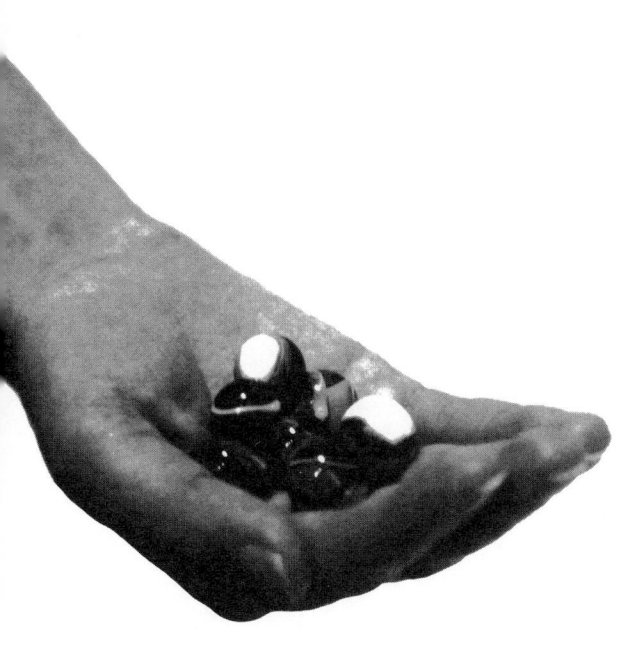

STEP SEVEN:
Maintaining Health, Independence and Social Integration

With the constant application and appreciation of the previous steps a 'well state' of mind and therefore well-being in life can be indefinitely maintained. In well-being physical health is as paramount as any other aspect in life, held equal to any other life enhancing activity.

It may also be found that in maintaining mental health you find it necessary to isolate problematic thought. These thoughts are identified along the way through the introspective recognition process that is becoming the foundation for your healthy life rhythm. I still find it necessary to identify those parts or attributes of myself that cause me mild distress in the relationships I have with people, partner, employment or environmental and future creativity. Those projections that originate from my childhood and social conditioning that actually hinder instead of help I am still constantly on the look out for. By projection I mean those sources of behaviour that originate in the acquired conditioning of formative years, which is then projected outward into relationships that happen to trigger particular contents of the mind or suppressed emotion. I am not obsessive in my self-observation as this could promote any number of neuroses, but through a consistent appreciation of the value of observation I am intuitively updated as to the validity and consequences of my thought. These self-appreciations and observations allow me in the long run to guide my life with less doubt and fear for the future. These anxieties I know would only contribute to creating circumstances that enhance my experiences of that fear and self-doubt. "What goes around comes around". If I act out of fear I create a fearful experience. If I recognise the creative process and origination of that anxiety I can liberate my consciousness of it, or at least learn to live with the fact that I have a tendency to behave in that way, and that I do not wish to carry on the same.

We can and do maintain mental health to the standards that we deem fit for ourselves. One problem with this self-standardisation is that without education or empirical observation we do not know what standards are healthy in the long run. Without sanity as a comparative guide, descending into impoverished mental health can be a slow ride into unconscious mental suicide, where we give up in delusive creativity and become strangers to ourselves.

This losing of self consciousness in slow, unconscious increments is not a desired outcome in maintaining mental health and is why I stress to those who have suffered this malaise the importance of applying self observation and introspective appreciation. Without these tools to self-awareness the descent into past behavioural patterns is an all too real phenomenon. It is probable that sufferers have been there before, again and again, feeling well for brief moments, only to wake up knowing that illness is once again the order of the day.

Swings of health from relative well-being into sickness on a regular basis betray an ungrounded personality. This is not the classic mood swing but is a condition where the sufferer is prone to getting ill within their self on a regular basis. This can be because this person is lacking a consistent constitution or self-belief mindset. By this consistent belief in self I mean those habitual, self-respective thoughts that are not self-derogatory in their nature. A process of investigation should be engaged in these cases not unlike attempts to discover allergies. As with dietary allergies the only way to find the source of the problem is to deny the person certain (dietary) influences. It could be that there is something in the mental health sufferer's immediate environment that triggers disorder. It could be people, partner, clandestine abuse and self-harm, drug abuse or the regular attempt to cope with recurring and traumatic memories. Something has got to give. Some aspect of the environment or self must be removed in order to reveal the healthier self. Without recognisable and safe aspects of self we can lose contact with our innate humanity; that part of us all which knows itself to be kind and loving, compassionate and capable of independent, healthy activity. This self-knowledge is not necessarily something that is held in the forefront of the mind but is a quality of life, something ineffably trustworthy; unspoken truths that people tend to take for granted and becoming unconscious of, end up unnecessarily selfish. This unconsciousness though is something most of humanity has in common and is rarely penetrated by curious minds intent on discovering the secrets within it.

When we trust that life is not the enemy and that it can be on our side we learn to work with those flows that we spent so much time going against in fruitless rebellion. We can become pleasantly surprised at the change in fortune presenting itself before the feet of our destiny.

Increased trust and the faith to instigate and initiate positive change in life both contribute directly to independent and confident decision making will power. Given the free will that got erroneously turned into self destructive mental illness you can re-educate your mind into self constructive, creative behaviour and before long be a pillar of strength to those who need empathy. You will no longer be looking to others for help, as you will not need it. Neither will you look upon yourself as the source of any pain as you will no longer self-conceive it nor manifest it in your life. There will not be relative pleasure to replace the old sufferings, but there will be the sense of an enduring well-being that gives you the assurance needed to fulfil those inclinations you know to be of your bettering.

With increased and inspired well-being you can integrate socially without fear of self opinionated and sometimes oppressive personalities shrinking you into self conscious anxiety. You can stand up for yourself; tackling any obstacle to self-learning that life throws at your confidence.

When you walk without fear or anxiety, without worries or self-concern you will tend to be unafraid of social integration as it is that humans tend to be social anyhow. Being sociable can be a consequence of being well in your self. Social acceptance is just a concept anyhow, tending to be mostly made up of collective anxieties that are not grounded in true social awareness. I for one will not be judged and stay quiet or be inhibited by invisible barriers that are not created by me. Your sense of what is right for you becomes enhanced by well-being. You will not find the need to dramatise yourself in well-being and neither will you want to act out what has been obsessively part of your mental make-up. Neither are you likely to be feebly subservient to authoritarian commands inflicted through emotionally vindictive esoteric or exoteric voices or convention.

Social integration comes naturally and is not a forced acquisition. When you are ready it will just be a part of your relaxed behaviour, in fact probably not something worth remarking about other than noticing you enjoy the experience. Also it is worth mentioning that you do not have to be social just to prove to yourself that you are OK and liked by people, as if these are factors in your well-being; you might just find yourself running manically around trying to fulfil an image that you think others hold about you. Believe me this is not pleasant, I've been there. Very quickly I forgot about my well-being when the priority in life seemed to me to be social interaction. I did not eat well, nor did I look after my emotional nature. I spent most of my time going with flows that I didn't even stop to ask myself if I liked. I became ungrounded very quickly and my poor diet contributed to an escalating sense of inability to get on with myself. I became unable to spend quality time alone or be content to amuse myself with things essentially good for exercising the independent freedom to be myself.

What can come to hamper the final release of mental illness are those idle reflections upon the past that sometimes trouble and destabilise our mental health. These are quite natural as they confirm one's present reality of well-being. Without well-being these reflections upon the past are impossible. When mentally disordered there is usually a full submersion in psycho-emotional suffering. When involved in sickness there is little distraction from it, especially not for casual introspections. Admittedly, those reminders are sometimes very strong and feelings associated with them can be just like the real thing, scary, anxious, manic, grand, etc, but with recognition comes relief, an application of the first step.

Try not to expect too much of yourself. This may have been a contributor to your original illness. No one is perfect and in my opinion ever can be. It is how we deal with the constant flux of the mind, the waves of movement and the evolving nature of our innate creativity that makes us who we are. Without this movement there would be no curiosity, no learning, the inability to let go of what no longer serves our bettering and there would be no comparative emotional cognition. Perhaps with absolute emancipation from the conditions of our humanity, in Buddha-hood or "Nirvana" there can be the free and unobstructed process of consciousness that seems to emulate eternity; a non-static state sometimes described as unconditionally loving. There is a place in human nature for this inviting union to which emancipation delivers us. But this one-ness is a far cry from those ordinary states of mind that sufferers of mental disorder crave, long and often die for to be reunited with. There is safety, security and identity in mental movement, and the knowledge that we are not alone in our ways, assured in our collective mind. Liberation from these ordinary conditions of human nature is a serious subject contained in much literature. This emancipating journey is usually embarked upon for one of two reasons. One is to perpetuate an escape from suppressed emotional denial and results in spiritual pride. The other is when desire or curiosity leads one to achieve a genuine, honest enquiry into the comparative truth or illusion regarding the human condition. The latter motive results in disillusionment.

Social integration is a very subjective topic and relies totally upon the inclination of the individual. How so ever you choose to interact with social environment is entirely your choice. Something you have had all along.

One step at a time These reviews act as concise reminders of the previous steps. They reiterate and hopefully embolden in the sufferer's mind the wisdom necessary for the liberation from mental disorder.

One step at a time, the SEVEN STEPS reviewed

STEP ONE *Problem Recognition and Identification*
Identifying and recognising that you have a problem is the first crucial step. It is sometimes helpful to take notes on your self-discoveries. This and communication with those we trust allows us to step aside from our problem. In stepping aside from our subjective life we can be objective about it instead, contributing directly to the practical affair of turning one's life around, from mental illness to mental wellbeing. This practicality promotes a grounded and self-aware approach to rediscovering innate humanity.

Whatever difficulties we may identify we know that from the very sense of difficulty is the knowledge that there is indeed a problem. Feelings of confusion and difficulty in maintaining "normal" functioning of the human condition as it is today is a sure sign of distress and perhaps mental illness. Talking to others about distress is an all too important first step in the right direction. Should you be hapless enough to have no one to trust then try practicing the methods in these steps to communicate coherently with your self. This coherence enhances objective introspection.

You must not fear being alone in dealing with your problem, even though at times you may feel lack of trust towards yourself. Being able to get the problems off our chests in worded form is extremely helpful. It is often the confused or insufficient communication in past traumatic situations that trigger disordered mental tendencies in the future. In writing down your thought processes comes the faith that you won't get lost or carried away by the very thoughts you are trying to observe; getting dragged into the same thought trains that contribute directly to your mental illness.

It is possible to affirm and so enhance those positive states of mind and emotion through faithfully thinking those states into being. Having these positive thought processes directly contributes to positive life experience. And so correspondingly if one has negative thought processes this contributes directly to negative life experiences. It is important to catch ourselves in whatever thought processes we have, being conscious and aware of the incidental content of our minds from moment to moment. This enables and facilitates conscious effort and introspective ability, making the process of conscious well-being a reality.

We can treat ourselves, correcting self-derogatory mental behaviour, freeing ourselves of often self-imposed disorder.

It is ultimately up to you to make the initial step in the right direction, deciding to be well. While there is some security, emotional investment or perceived benefit in remaining unwell you will continue being mentally unfit.

You must remember that you are not alone in your heart. There are ways to help our selves no matter how severe problems appear to be. Finding out through yourself or others how it was that you became unwell you will be left knowing how it is that you can become well. These realisations come naturally in the process of self-awareness that leads to future well-being.

STEP TWO *Acceptance and Resolution*

It is imperative that you accept that there is a problem, that something is not quite right about your mental behaviour. Any stubbornness or obstinacy towards allowing yourself to realise the evident problem will only hinder your progress towards a healthier future. With acceptance you will find the impetus that motivates you to do something positive about your behaviour. This takes courage in the outset but once on the road to well-being there will be no stopping you.

Remember that you are not alone in your pains, although often it may feel that way. Be assured that others have been there before and have sorted themselves out, even if you are actually on your own.

It is important to realise that getting well does not contain persistent thoughts of comparing your present behaviour to the past. Once you have the confidence to deal with the past you can reflect on your previous states of living and mind. Comparing your behaviour to the past will at this stage only compromise your efforts in these initial steps toward self-confidence.

Acceptance soon leads to the resolve to make actual steps in altering your way of life. Resolve is the practical side to the somewhat psychological art of acceptance. Affirmations often offer the positivity to carry on in this time of uncertainty, where you may not always be so sure of your future. *"I am going to be well". "I am going to better myself every day". "I don't want to be sick any more"*. These are powerful statements that are not easily forgotten.

STEP THREE *Tolerance and Problem Isolation*

Partially recognising or momentarily observing the manifestation of your particular mental illness is a good start in the continuous process of introspection. Exercise in this activity of self-awareness increases confidence in self. As knowledge of self increases the practical ability to respond and to ultimately apply self-learned solutions to your own problems becomes easier. This is your ability to respond, your responsibility.

Isolating in your mind mental struggle helps you to step out of the involvement with those thoughts, driving a wedge in between who you truly are and what is not a healthy state of mind. Associating one's self with well mental behaviour is thus disassociating oneself from the illness. This practice helps to fade the unhealthy aspect into ultimate insignificance as you progress towards absolute health. Dissociation requires of one to have accepted the original problem and is not a denial of the problem. It is recognition that allows this dissociation to take place.

Dwelling in thoughts that are self-derogatory lead one to insecure, unconfident and depressive states of the heart and mind.

The process of thought recognition and introspection tends one towards the goal of awareness and self-wisdom, providing one with emotional maturity and a growing confidence. These attributes are invaluable in today's social drama.

STEP FOUR *Physical Health Consequences*

It is upon repetitious body language and posture that our mental disorders depend. If you change the body language you will change the superficial state of the mind. Because the mind superficially identifies with and through the body it uses body posture and physical movement as the foundation for it's mental formation and expression.

Caring for the mind and body as co-dependent qualities of the human condition brings one to the awareness that a healthy body means a healthy mind. Eating healthy foods for example promotes the healthy welfare of the body.

It is only the fear of change that stops one from making the necessary steps into more fulfilling processes of increasing health and well-being. Allow yourself to move away from the security in feelings of painful familiarity.

Be vigilant in your self and in stepping outside of your self in order to observe your own behaviour. Make mental or written notes of repetitious behaviour so that you can extract valuable information that may help you to exact and apply useful changes. This will ultimately change your mind.

Bring self-control into your life, bodily functions and interactions. Being controlled by past emotional distress only brings the past into an uncomfortable present. Instead you can when you feel comfortable view the past from a secure present. This will promote the confidence to release those problematic mental formations and feelings through communication.

STEP FIVE *Stimulus replacement, encouraging esteem and motivation*

Psychological problems have the tendency to find ways of surviving, constantly adapting to changes in circumstance. This contributes to the illusion that there can be no reprieve from your confusion. It is an illusion and you can do something to alter mental circumstance and perception of environmental conditions.

Enjoying the attention received whilst suffering from illness is a way of perpetuating sickness, affirming one's identification and association with disorder.

Stepping beyond the relative security of emotional and psychological distress, successfully depleting the power of sickness over your confident independence will often leave you feeling a little empty. This is quite normal and is part of the adjustment process as you pass through from one psychological identification or mindset and into another. This is literally changing your mind.

Associations with healthier mindsets contribute directly to well-being. One example of a healthier mindset would be the application of the affirmation to better one's self on a day-to-day basis.

Accumulating confidence through successfully engaging in creative and independent endeavour is another major contributor to healthy mentality. Achieving a healthier diet and living with the recognition that life can be lived without old sufferable habits are the boldest steps toward a progressively healthy attitude. Changing the day-to-day content of our minds changes the way we see the world and ourselves in it. It changes our belief systems, motivation, encouragement and self-respect. It is possible through replacement of the old with the new to create a healthier mindset, to live beyond the relative security of the past and it's pain.

Those who have suffered psychological breakdown, upheaval or confusion have the unique moment in life to change their minds, changing their outlook, aims and even future achievements. Confronting fear of change can be a life long challenge and to me is certainly the most fulfilling pursuit, giving opportunities I never thought I would experience, and a life without regret.

Make positive plans for the future. They become goals that keep you grounded in the present. It is just as important to know what you don't want as to know what you do want; they are both perspectives giving creative direction to an otherwise hapless existence.

STEP SIX *Overcoming diagnosis, institutionalisation, medication and social stigma*

Diagnosis can become a source of identity, a label providing some kind of security. At least you can know who you are in terms of diagnosis. To face the unknown can appear intimidating and this fear can contribute to the return of mental disorder.

There are different kinds of institutionalisation. Such as those through medication, social services, social stigma and those of abusive, self-deluding security psychosis. It is important to consider that perhaps you contribute psychosomatically to your own mental welfare. One's disorder is caused and self created out of traumatic choice or else it is a result of an unfortunate bio-clinical deficiency.

A good affirmation is not considering one's self to be sick. The absence of self-detrimental belief systems is actually an affirmation of positive mental attitude.

Reducing and finally ending medication when there can be found no reason to continue is an empowering reclamation of independence. You are the source of your empowerment.

Cutting out medication goes hand in hand with a growing confidence in well-being.

It is important not to forget that social services are an excellent source of encouragement and therapy. Rebellion against this service could be a neglect of your welfare. Ultimately though there comes a time when through health it is natural to reject that which you no longer need.

The longer that you leave your life in the hands of rules

and regulations, external services or institutions the more your mind and therefore your body associate these conditions with normality, making it harder to free one's self from the very system that helped.

Once you start integrating with society with a well and healthy demeanour people will be surprised and astonished to hear that you were once unwell. This is progress. It is you who have had these unique experiences of despair or mental trauma that will then be able to live with a deeper appreciation of the goodness that life offers in freedom from mental tribulation.

Moments of candid honesty help to clear your heart and mind of any residual self-conscious inhibitions borne of the past.

Confidence can be found in many things the more aware you are prepared to be of yourself and the directions that you wish to take in the present.

STEP SEVEN Maintaining health, independence and social integration

Self-appreciation and observation act as guides in life, reducing self-doubt and contributing to fearlessness.

If I act out of fear I create a fearful experience. If I can recognise this creative process I can use it to my own benefit. By creating positive phenomena about myself within my environment I will achieve well-being.

We maintain mental health to the standards that we deem fit for ourselves. A problem with this self-standardisation is that without education or an empirical appreciation of past experience it is not possible to know what standard is healthy or contributes positively to our life.

The importance of applying self-observation and of having introspective appreciation becomes apparent when it is realised that they are tools for self-awareness. That they can halt any return to self-depreciative behaviour or mental disorder.

Swings of health from relative well-being into sickness on a regular basis betray an ungrounded personality. A person lacking consistent constitution, positive self-belief, self-respect or self initiated, structured and relaxed daily routine.

We can begin to trust in the life around us, that it can be our friend if that is how we are prepared to see it and relate to it. Increased trust and the faith to initiate positive changes in our lives both contribute to independent and confident decision making will power.

You can stand up for yourself, tackling any obstacle to self-learning that life throws at your confidence.

Having the ability to be sociable when it pleases you is a consequence of well-being. There is not the need to dramatise yourself in well-being. Social integration comes naturally and is not a forced acquisition. Try not to expect too much of yourself.

No one is perfect. It is how we deal with the constant flux of the mind and the evolving nature of our innate creativity that makes us who we are.

GOOD LUCK!

GLOSSARY OF TERMS

Emotive mind – Those feelings we identify through the inner observation of our minds. E.g. one does not have to wait until a violent outburst occurs to know that one is feeling angry. The anger can be noted as an emotive presence from the vantage point of introspective observation, prior to any necessary or unnecessary aggressive expression.

Esoteric – Those things that originate from within an organism.

Exoteric – Those things that result from causes external to an organism.

Obsessive thought formation – This is the self-generation of thoughts that are of some comfort to the thinker. They can be fantastical in nature or in the form of recurrent daydreaming. One becomes obsessed with the content of thought until the thought itself feels as though it is the possessor of the personality. There then ensues the compulsion to think that thing, over and over.

Sectional environment – The consequences of being Sectioned under the Mental Health Act. It is in the form of restricted freedom for safety reasons, or the conditional environment of the outpatient.

Self-created security neurosis – The imposition òf self-conceived conditions that actually restrict personal freedom, applied in order to remain in known and apparently safe or secure mindsets. Pain can be conceived as safe as it does not confront the person with the unknown, which may actually be a more fulfilling and emotionally liberated condition.

Self-deluding security psychosis – The escalation of security neurosis. If not confronted neurotic mentality can evolve into delusive thought; a psychosis that eventually finds expression through disordered behaviour.